Roman Mythology

A Guide to Roman History, Gods, and Mythology

Peter Collins

Table of Contents

Introduction 1

Chapter 1: The Gods and Goddesses of Rome 7

Chapter 2: The Demigods of Rome 20

Chapter 3: The Famous Stories of Roman Mythology 28

Chapter 4: The Influences of Greek Mythology on Roman Mythology 39

Chapter 5: How the Gods Were Worshiped in Ancient Rome . 47

Chapter 6: Where You Can Still See Roman Mythology's Influence Today 59

Conclusion 64

References 68

Introduction

Ancient Rome and its mythology comprise an era, and component, of history that seems to pique everybody's interest at some point or other. And the bonus is that you can never be too early nor too late in learning about it! In this particular book you will find out the basics of Roman mythology, how it affected the lives of the ancient Romans, and even the ways in which some aspects of their mythology have trickled down into modern Western society. The aim is to leave you with a well-rounded idea of the core elements of Roman mythology: Who were the gods, goddesses, and demigods? Why were they worshiped? And what stories existed of them? It is important to note now that there existed more gods of Rome than will be mentioned here, and similarly, there are numerous more mythological stories of their deeds than we will have time to cover. Many years could be spent dedicated to studying the different gods and stories of Ancient Rome. So, the aim with this book is to simply give you the rundown of the most prominent and important—the ones the Romans themselves would have also focused on the most.

Who Were the Romans?

It is practically inconceivable in Western society to not have heard of, and have some basic knowledge about, the ancient Romans. What constituted a Roman varied somewhat over the course of Roman history, as they expanded and became an Empire instead of a Republic. In earlier times, to be considered a Roman you would have to be born in Rome or one of its closely neighboring settlements. Later, as the Roman Empire set out and expanded, more people would have been classed as Roman, although being born within the Empire did not automatically make you so.

Romans are well-known for being the first people to build such impressive infrastructure as proper roads. Many places that were under the rule of the Roman Empire at some point or other in the past still have roads in use today that follow the old Roman roads. Other industrious exploits of the Romans consisted of bathhouses and aqueducts. They were among the first civilizations to understand the need for hygienic cleanliness and clean water, although it is believed that they wouldn't have understood the actual science behind it all. Bathhouses were available to every Roman, regardless of class and status, as they were aware that one dirty person could quickly cause the downfall of the many. Similarly, aqueducts often stretched the width and length of Roman settlements to ensure that all the people were able to access clean water as needed.

The Romans were also a rather fun and sporting peoples. Within their vast repertoire of events and festivals, they took part in and performed in the well-documented gladiatorial games and chariot races. Sometimes these events may have been used to disadvantage the previous occupants of the area, and to draw the attention of the Roman people away from any less preferable aspects of life, thus decreasing the chance of uprisings and dissent. However, wherever the Romans went, they did still bring the opportunity of increased health and well-being to those they conquered.

This was all on top of their religious beliefs and behaviors, which would have been imbued into almost every aspect of their culture.

What Does "Mythology" Mean?

"Mythology" refers to the scholastic interpretation of the hallowed stories of ancient civilizations and cultures. The word itself stems from the Greek "mythos," meaning "story of the people," and the word "logos," meaning "word" or "speech." Together it means "spoken tales of the people," which is a fantastic meaning since most myths did not start out being written down. Based on cave paintings and other very early art forms made by homo sapiens, it appears that ever since man was able to have complex thoughts, mythology has existed. This is almost entirely due to the fact that myths were used by all civilizations to help them explain and understand how the world around them worked, and also why people were the way they were. Myths were used to explain away such things as: why we experience suffering, what it means to be a good person or a bad person, the cycle of life and death, and even the origin of place names and events. Essentially, mythologies were the method of keeping everyone sane when there wasn't enough knowledge of science to help explain these things instead.

Myths all end up falling into one of a very few categories. For the most part, myths can either be deemed historical myths or etiological myths. In the case of historical myths, this is when someone or a group of people take a real historical event and build upon it to make it a more supernatural and heroic situation than it really would have been. Etiological myths, on the other hand, are those that are completely made up but have the important role of helping the masses understand the processes of the world they are living in. An example of the first is the fall of Troy, while an example of the latter is the myth of Proserpina and Pluto, which you will find out more about later in this book.

In all mythologies, especially throughout the Mediterranean, you will find many of the same components. All will contain gods and goddesses, and in most cases—as with the Romans and the Greeks—there will also be demigods: half mortal, half god, worshiped by the people as heroes. Other supernatural beings are also commonplace throughout these tales. In many, you will tend to come across nymphs, satyrs, and other humanoid elemental creatures. Unique names and slight differences in characterization do arise from culture to culture, but the bare essentials are always more or less the same.

What You Can Expect to Learn

You need to get into the mindset now, before you set out reading, of just how integrated the ancient religion was with all the other elements of Roman life. It will be best if you read on with the knowledge already established that these people saw worshiping the gods as *the* most important part of their lives. Sure, from time to time a leader would arise who was a little more skeptical of the need for such devout behavior in all that they did, but even these men would ultimately respect the ways and traditions of their people. As you read, think about how this level of devotion would have influenced the way in which people acted towards each other and how this could have affected the success of the Romans as a whole.

Additionally, to be able to fully comprehend the scope of Roman mythology you will need to understand that the Romans did not come up with all these deities and stories by themselves. A lot of the basics of their religion were copied from other cultures, most notably the Greeks. This will be covered in more depth as you read on, but be sure to know that you are likely to see many more similarities between the two mythologies than you see differences!

As you read this book you will notice that the same collection of names seem to pop up over and over again. Mentions of Jupiter will likely be the most common, as he was seen as the father and king of the gods, and thus also of Rome, resulting in him being present throughout nearly everything they did. Other major players consisted of demigods such as Aeneas and Hercules, as well as historical figures like Julius Caesar, Augustus Caesar, and Cicero—two of which claimed divinity to themselves and the other ensured strict religious practices from the Roman people under his influence.

The likelihood is that you will come across some things in this book that you've heard about somewhere else before, but hopefully by the time you've finished reading you will have discovered a thing or two! Not only that, but by the end of this book, ideally your interest in Roman mythology will have expanded and you will be eager to go on and develop your knowledge in more specific and specialized areas of the world of ancient Roman mythology.

Chapter 1: The Gods and Goddesses of Rome

According to the myths, when the gods and goddesses first came into existence, the earliest Romans initially believed there to have been only four of them, Jupiter and his sisters: Juno, Vesta, and Ceres. These four were the children of two Titans: Saturn, the Titan of Time, and Ops (or Opis), the Goddess of the Earth. Through the leadership of Jupiter, they would rid the world of the tyranny of the Titans. The full story about this will be covered later in this book. In later editions of the origins of the gods, the gods Neptune and Pluto were changed to be recognized as the brothers of Jupiter instead of his sons. This likely happened in line with influences coming in from Greece, which will be discussed in more depth later on. Regardless of the change to his brothers, according to the myths as time went on, Jupiter would then go on to sire the majority of the rest of the Roman pantheon.

As with every other civilization and culture, these gods and goddesses existed to fill the void that was created by logical thought without the presence of science. They were designed to help give meaning to what can be a very confusing world, and to give people hope even when times look dire. Together, the first six divine entities covered the core aspects of what makes up the world and what it means to be human: the sky, the sea, growth, warmth, family, and death.

Vesta the Goddess of the Hearth and Ceres the Goddess of Agriculture

Outside of Juno, these goddesses were the only sisters of Jupiter. Vesta was known as the Goddess of the Hearth. Rome itself had what they called "Vestal Virgins," priestesses who were in charge of Rome's sacred fire—a fire that was not permitted to be extinguished. This college of priestesses was so particular and important to the Romans' way of life that the women would swear an oath of chastity and were not permitted to marry. This way they were able to devote all their time to the study and performance of the correct Vestal rituals—something no male priest was allowed involvement in.

Ceres was the Goddess of Agriculture. She was the mother of Proserpina, who was the Goddess of Seasonal Agriculture, with whom she presided over all forms of growth. Ceres was worshiped largely through annual festivals, in both the spring and at the time of harvest. Some sources claim that Ceres would also be prayed to during marriage and funeral rites. This may have been since she could be seen as a sign of new life, and in other instances was also often shown to be mourning, since she would lose her daughter to the Underworld for months at a time.

Besides these key aspects of their divinity, neither of these goddesses played too large a part in Roman mythology. Essentially, they were the quiet support characters to their brothers, while making sure that the world kept ticking along as it should.

Neptune: God of the Sea

The Roman god Neptune was known for being the God of the Sea. He would have also been considered the God of Freshwater, and generally was seen as having control over all types of water, from trickling streams to the oceans themselves. As with many of the gods and goddesses, he had a few additional side gigs, dabbling here and there in other affairs such as winds, storms, and horse racing.

Never revered as a ruling god, simply as an immensely powerful one, Neptune was said to have spent most of his time at his home, in a golden palace under the waves of the Mediterranean Sea, with his wife and sons. His wife was Salacia, the Goddess of Salt Waters, while his sons included the somewhat known Triton, also a god of the sea like his father.

The key myth surrounding Neptune is that he decided the shape of the world as the Romans knew it to be. According to the tales, Neptune wielded his power over all waters to shape the sea beds, the shores, and even the mountains and valleys by way of his control over rivers. Outside of this, Neptune is much more of a supporting character in most myths.

Despite Neptune's absence in some earlier versions of the pantheon, in the most widely accepted and recounted versions of the tales of the gods, Neptune was considered a brother to the King of the Gods. This could be a side effect of the influences of Greek mythology that will be discussed in more depth later, but essentially it can be assumed as a result of the fact that Poseidon (Neptune's Greek counterpart) was unfailingly known as the brother of the Greek god Zeus (Jupiter's counterpart).

Pluto: God of the Underworld

Pluto was the Roman God of the Dead and Lord of the Underworld. He was also considered the God of Wealth, largely due to the fact that most precious ores are found underground. For this reason he also tended to be conflated with Plouton, the Lord of Wealth, who was a very early form of Roman deity. Additionally, in the same boat as Neptune, Pluto was not always necessarily considered a brother of Jupiter, but it is as a brother that he became most commonly known. Pluto was one of the few major gods that had no religious festivals in his honor. There has been some speculation over why, particularly since he was the god of such an important aspect of life. Most scholars have come to agree that it was most likely to maintain the sense of mystery that Pluto imbued in the people.

Depictions of Pluto have a tendency to show him wearing a warrior's helm. In art forms outside of statues, he can also be seen with Kerebos, reclined in a chariot, and often with a staff.

Pluto was said to have lived a lonely existence in the shadowy realm of the dead, found almost always residing in his dreary palace. His only real companion was his three-headed dog, Kerebos, who acted as both his pet and the guardian of the underworld. The way in which Pluto was portrayed also implies that he had little to no interest in the land of the living, nor the affairs of the other gods. Eventually he would make Ceres' only daughter, Proserpina, his wife—against her wishes—and after making agreements with Jupiter, he would be permitted to keep her with him for half the year. Some ancient sources do imply that Pluto had children, although none have been found to really specify who. The best guess that has been made over the years since is that he is likely the father of the Furies, a group of vengeful divine entities that also lived within the shadows of the underworld.

The King and Queen of the Gods: Jupiter and Juno

Jupiter

Jupiter was known as both the father and the king of the gods of Rome. He was also directly linked to Rome itself, initially through his supposed communications and negotiations with King Numa in the early ages of the city. According to this particular myth, it was these interactions that granted the Romans the rights of the *imperium*—the ability to use "absolute power" over people. It was natural for the Romans to choose Jupiter as their representative divine entity and conjure up these stories of him interacting with early Romans, particularly since he was depicted as a natural leader and was also deemed the most powerful over the other gods and goddesses—in the same way that the Romans tended to see themselves as the forerunners of the time, and ultimately also the most powerful of their contemporaries.

Jupiter is rarely seen portrayed in any sort of juvenile state, and some sources claim that there was little to no literature on his origins until the introduction of mythical tales of the equivalent gods of Greece. His depictions usually involve him being seated on a throne while holding a staff and a scepter. In some art he is also shown wielding lightning bolts, which were his personal weapon as God of the Sky.

Juno

As mentioned, Juno was nearly always depicted as a sister of Jupiter, even since some of the earliest retellings of the origins of the gods. She seems to have appeared in a time before even Neptune and Pluto were seen as brothers and not the children of Jupiter. However, even Juno did not necessarily come on the scene with the Roman people at the same time as Jupiter. According to a source in Livy, who claims to recall the words of Marcus Furius Camillus after the sacking of Rome by the Gauls in 390 BC, Juno had only in somewhat recent—potentially even living—memory become fully recognized as a goddess of Rome. Regardless of where she may have originated from, she still went on to be cemented in a lofty position among the Roman pantheon, with the Roman people believing her to be the mother of many of their other gods and goddesses.

In terms of her role as a standalone goddess, Juno was referred to as the Goddess of Marriage and Family. She was also seen as a Goddess of Love and the Home, indicating that the form of love she governed over was that of a love between spouses, or parents and children. She was also seen as a protector of the state of

Rome and a champion of women, particularly those who were treated poorly by men.

Juno was usually depicted in a mature manner, still classically beautiful and stunning, but not overly youthful. She was often seen dressed in militaristic clothing and holding a staff or a spear. The staff may have been to symbolize her role as the Queen of the Gods, whilst the other militaristic aspects were to distinguish her as Roman and make it clear that she was a different goddess from the Greek goddess Hera (otherwise known as her counterpart).

The Children of Jupiter

For the most part, the generally well-known gods and goddesses of the ancient Roman pantheon in some way come back to being born of Jupiter. This is less the case for a couple of them—most notably his siblings—but otherwise it tends to follow suit, therefore surprising no one that Jupiter is often referred to as the father of all gods by the Romans themselves. On the other hand, there are a few gods and goddesses who are not the direct children of Jupiter, but are instead his grandchildren or similar alternative relatives.

With Juno

Of Jupiter's (at least) ten divine children (there were plenty more in the form of demigods), his wife Juno was the mother of four. Her four children consisted of: Mars (the God of War), Vulcan (the God of Fire), Bellona (the Goddess of War), and Juventas (the Goddess of Youth).

According to the myths, Mars is the father of the demigods Romulus and Remus, who were the founders of the city of Rome. He was also a lover of Venus and is said to have sired the god Cupid, the God of Desire, through her. Vulcan also has a close link to Venus. He was meant to be her husband, but they had no children together because Venus had a preference for Mars.

Bellona and Juventas are not as well recorded as their brothers and did not receive any of the specific public worship that the gods did. It seems this was a bit of a running theme within the Roman pantheon. Very few goddesses got dedicated annual events and rites, outside of Juno, Ceres, and possibly Venus.

Juno had no children with anyone besides Jupiter. This was entirely a result of a crucial element of how she was perceived as a goddess and the fact that she was the Goddess of Marriage and Family. These factors meant that she had to be intimately faithful to her husband for all eternity. Because of how she is and must be, it is not all that shocking that in many myths she is more than a little upset when she discovers her husband's infidelity—although, more often than not, she would take it out on either the other woman, any children involved, or both. A major example of this is the jealousy that she held towards both Hercules and Aeneas—Hercules because he was a son of Jupiter, Aeneas because through him Rome would be founded, which meant that Jupiter's attention would be spread even more thinly.

Via other lovers

Jupiter had numerous other lovers according to the myths, although not all his sexual encounters resulted in any children—god, demigod, or otherwise. Those that did result in the birth of other gods generally came from his interactions with other divine entities. From the Titan Metis, he fathered Minerva, the Goddess of Wisdom. The story of Minerva follows the lines of the Greek myth of Athena almost exactly. Her father ate her mother out of fear that the child she was pregnant with would be more powerful than him. After her birth, Jupiter experienced agonizing pain, to the degree that he asked his son Vulcan to break open his head with a hammer from his forge. When his son did so, Minerva emerged from the split in Jupiter's head, fully grown and clothed in battle armor. Jupiter did not need to worry about being overthrown by his daughter; she was a powerful goddess in her own right but much more focused on strategic planning than on overthrowing anyone. Regardless, she would still help rule, as she was a part of the Capitoline Triad that also included Jupiter and Juno, which together oversaw the skies. Initially, the Triad was made up of Jupiter, Mars, and Quirinus (the deified form of Romulus, the founder of Rome), but with time Minerva would replace Mars because she was also a Goddess of War, but through her wisdom was able to provide more useful insight than her half-brother.

Another time, Maia, the daughter of a Titan, stole the gaze of Jupiter. From this coupling, the god Mercury, the Messenger God, was conceived. Mercury was the only god that could exist equally in both the heavens above and the underworld. Pluto himself was said not to be able to leave the underworld for too lengthy periods of time, and all the other gods were not able to enter it. Proserpina is the only other deity to eventually have the ability to cross "freely" between the two planes of existence, and this was only because Pluto forced her into the underworld in the first place.

There are two additional Roman goddesses, beyond Juno, with whom Jupiter fathered gods and goddesses. The first of these is one of his other sisters, Ceres. Together they were the parents of Proserpina, the Goddess of Seasonal Agriculture. Proserpina would go on to live in the underworld with her husband Pluto. The story goes that her mother is so sad during the months that her daughter is locked away from her that she permits nothing to grow, and it is only during the spring and summer—when they are reunited—that the world is allowed to grow once again. The other goddess is Latona, the Goddess of Motherhood. She is the mother of Apollo and Diana, the God of the Sun and the Goddess of the Moon. Apollo is also known for being the God of Poetry, Music, and Archery. It is of little surprise, therefore, that Apollo is often depicted in relation to arts and culture, sometimes even in modern contexts. Diana, on the other hand, was revered as also being the Goddess of Fertility, Hunting, and Wild Animals. Seen as a virginal goddess, she was often depicted as having a group of huntresses with her, all of whom had also sworn an oath of chastity. Young women would pray to her while they were unwed.

The creation of Bacchus, the God of Wine, is an odd one if you are to follow the rules of producing a god versus a demigod. This is because Bacchus was the son of a mortal woman, Semele, and yet he would still go on to be deemed a god. The only real explanation for this sits in Greek mythology, where Hestia (Ceres) gives up her place as a major god in order for Dionysus (Bacchus) to become one instead.

And so, you can see that the vast majority of the major gods of the Roman pantheon were of Jupiter, undoubtedly securing his place as the father of the gods of Rome.

Gods and Goddesses not sired by Jupiter

Some gods and goddesses were not the result of Jupiter's sexual exploits, but they are few and far between outside of his siblings. One major goddess to whom Jupiter is not always attributed as her father, is Venus, the Goddess of Love and Beauty. Venus is instead more often referred to as the daughter of a more primal Roman god—Caelus—although some may argue that he is simply an earlier version of the god that went on to be Jupiter. While Venus is a Goddess of Love, just as Juno is, the forms of love she covers is where it differs. Venus was used to indicate a most lustful love, whereas Juno would have been called upon in matters of bonding that did not involve the physical side of things.

The only other somewhat commonly known god not directly born of Jupiter is Cupid. As mentioned before, Cupid, the God of Desire, is instead the sole child of Mars and Venus. In this way, although he was not sired by Jupiter himself, you could still claim he is *of* Jupiter, since the God of the Sky is technically his paternal grandfather. Not only that, but by being with Mars, and becoming the mother of Cupid, Venus had technically asserted her position within the Roman pantheon, and therefore under Jupiter's rule.

Chapter 2: The Demigods of Rome

Who Were the Demigods?

Demigods were almost always the result of sexual relations between a god and a mortal. In nearly every case they became, and were later revered as, heroes of their age. Alternately, in the few instances that a person was considered a demigod but had not been conceived this way, it was likely because they had some other traits which ultimately led them to either be deified by the Gods themselves, and brought up to the heavens above upon death, or to be deified by the people, although this also tended to happen after the death of the person.

For the most part, Jupiter played the biggest part in fathering the demigods of the myths. Through his actions with mortal women like Alcmene and Danae, we gained the stories of heroes like Hercules and Perseus. What seems quite telling is that Jupiter's supposedly siring all the demigods is a fact realistically attributed to Greek myths in the first place. As a result, many more such as Amphion, Minos, Rhadamanthus, and Sarpedon have been at one time or another implied to have been fathered by Jupiter while most sources still focus on them being the children of Zeus. It is because of this intense cultural mingling that we have to also be careful about those whom we claim Jupiter to have slept with, as it is likely that Jupiter was not quite as promiscuous as Zeus was made out to be. Just because *much* of the Greek source material was co-opted into Roman mythology does not mean that *all* of it was.

Some of the other gods and goddesses had a hand in creating demigods here and there. Venus was the supposed mother of Aeneas, and while Mars didn't father more than the two demigods, his actions turned out to be immensely important in the religious history of the Romans. His sons Romulus and Remus would be cited as the reason Rome would go on to become the powerhouse that it became.

Demigods born of gods and goddesses always possessed at least a few of the same characteristics. They would always be brave, although they would also often have a tendency to be boastful. The majority of them also had the benefit of supernatural levels of strength, although some more than others. Others were blessed with full or partial immortality, however it tended to be the case that all the demigods joined the gods in the skies above upon their deaths and that very few had to move on to the underworld. Clearly, it was almost always the case that the demigods could not be perfect; that was reserved for the gods and goddesses, and it helped maintain a sense of humanity in the heroes. Importantly, each hero had at least one flaw to counter their extraordinary strengths. This varied from hero to hero. For some it was a physical downfall, others it was more personality-based, and yet others would experience their downfall as the result of their close relationship with another—for example, a twin brother.

It is largely due to the latter method of "creating" a demigod that at some point just prior to and during the rise of the Roman Empire it became not uncommon for the emperor to be considered a demigod—or even a god—in some way. This was not always the case, but can be seen most prominently during the reign of Julius Caesar and Caesar Augustus, both of whom have not only been considered demigods, but in some cases are referred to as being gods of the Roman pantheon upon their deaths. This act of revering them alongside the demigods of mythology would have stemmed from the fact that these were two men who possessed immense power in the eyes of the people, and so the following implication that their power was in some way bestowed upon them by the gods would have arisen.

Romulus and Remus

The twins Romulus and Remus were born of a mortal Vestal Virgin, Rhea Silvia (who also happened to be the daughter of King Numitor) and the god Mars. Despite the best efforts of their great-uncle to have them killed, eventually they would go on to found Rome, although on completion of the city one would kill the other, and this would become known as the very first day of Rome's existence. While perhaps not Rome's most famous or memorable demigods, they were certainly the most important within ancient Roman culture.

Since the earliest depictions of the pair, they are always shown to be suckling at a wolf's teat. This was because of the abnormal childhood they experienced as a result of the wrath of their great-uncle, who was king of the lands at the time, but that will be discussed in more detail later in this book.

Hercules

Hercules was the son of Jupiter and Alcmene, a mortal woman. His story is directly adapted from the Greek Heracles—same origins, same struggles and triumphs—all just with a little extra Roman flair thrown in for good measure.

A man of immense strength, Hercules was constantly being messed around with by the actions of a jealous Juno who was unimpressed that Jupiter had sired yet another bastard demigod. Hercules married and had five children with his wife, Megara. However, he was also prone to a blinding rage, induced by the will of Juno, and in one of these fits the myths claim he killed his whole family. He was remorseful of the event and looked to Apollo for guidance. The deeds he did in order to attempt to absolve himself and help him through his grief became known as the Labors of Hercules.

Aeneas

Aeneas was the son of Venus and the mortal man Anchises. The myth surrounding Aeneas encourages the Romans to unlearn the old Greek ways and instead, embrace what it means to be a Roman. It is quite likely, therefore, that Aeneas was chosen as a forefather of Rome because, by being a Trojan, he was already a natural enemy of the Greeks and so was one step removed from their culture.

He was one of the heroes of Troy, connected to the royal line, who escaped as the city burned, leading a shipload of other survivors behind him. He went on to settle the refugee Trojans in Latium, wed the daughter of the king there, and through his line Romulus and Remus would rise to found Rome.

Why Were Demigods Important?

The importance of demigods comes largely from the fact that they were half mortal. By having these heroes directly tethered to the world of man it would have allowed the Roman people to be inspired by their stories and may have helped guide Roman citizens towards being better people. While the average person couldn't be expected to perform the same feats as Hercules, they would have been able to appreciate where there were similarities between their own lives and the things experienced by the demigods. For example, if a demigod lost a loved one and was struggling with the suffering that they were feeling, the average Roman would be able to easily associate their own life experiences with that. Therefore, when the hero managed to overcome their grief and perhaps even improve upon something because of it, a Roman hearing the story would likely think to apply similar actions to their own situation.

Political Leaders Worshiped as Demigods

Especially when considering that the members of the Roman pantheon were in many ways exaggerated human beings, it is not hard to believe that the everyday people of ancient Rome, watching the successful acts of their leaders, generals, and the like, would have willingly applied characteristics of divinity to them. Similarly, it becomes easier to reconcile that leaders and generals would claim these characteristics for themselves and the people would not bat an eyelid. It was often suggested in religious laws that when it came to times of worship, to include in your prayers people who possessed positive traits that would please the gods, that they could then receive higher favor with the gods. It is not shocking, therefore, that many Roman leaders just so happened to fit the mold of at least some of these characteristics.

In the case of Julius Caesar, we have an example of a mortal who laid claims to a lineage from the gods. He was said to claim that he was a descendant of the line of Venus and Aeneas, therefore linking himself to the very roots of Rome. As he rose to higher and higher levels of power, Caesar began to try and lay into his position as a demigod himself with ever increasing acts of self-importance. Ultimately, he even had priests assigned to him during his lifetime, an attempt to convince the people that he was in fact a god. But it was not until after he was assassinated that he was actually deified—to the level of a god of Rome, no less.

Augustus Caesar was a slightly different story. He was adopted as Julius Caesar's heir by Caesar himself, not all that much prior to his death. After the assassination of Julius, Augustus (at this point called Octavian) helped lead the battle against the schemers alongside Mark Anthony, Julius Caesar's cousin. Once that was solved, Augustus turned on Mark Anthony due to his alliance with Cleopatra of Egypt, defeated the both of them and returned victorious to Rome. With all that said and done, he went ahead with deifying Julius Caesar, then announced that this meant he was the son of a god, and changed his name to Augustus Caesar, Emperor. This was the beginning of the Roman Empire and a sure start to the political leaders of Rome being seen as, or at least on par with, demigods.

Chapter 3: The Famous Stories of Roman Mythology

The Origins of Jupiter

Jupiter's origin story is exactly the same as the Greek god Zeus'. It is probable that Jupiter did not have an origin story until the introduction of Greek influences. Regardless, this is how it goes.

At the beginning of time there were the Titans. They ruled the earth and the sky above. Not all were malicious, but many could easily be. Jupiter was born of the titans Saturn and Ops. Saturn was aware of a prophecy that claimed a child of his would usurp him as the lord of the skies, and so as Ops birthed each of his children, Saturn swallowed them whole. When the time came for Jupiter to be born, Ops hid him and instead provided Saturn with a rock swaddled in blankets. Since Saturn ate it whole, he did not notice that it was not a baby.

Jupiter then grew and plotted. All the while his father was experiencing terrible indigestion. Eventually, Saturn could think of no other solution than to throw up, ejecting his five other children in the process. Jupiter seized the opportunity of his freed brothers and sisters to defeat his father and take his fated place as King of the Gods.

Jupiter Meets the Romans

The second ruler of Rome, King Numa, was the first to introduce Jupiter himself to the Roman people. Supposedly, during a particularly severe time of strife, Numa managed to get an audience with the God of the Sky, by tricking two lesser gods into summoning Jupiter to a meeting place. Jupiter promised only to help the king and his people if they agreed to worship him in the manner that he desired.

Once that agreement was all ironed out, Jupiter taught Numa methods of avoiding lightning bolts, the reason Numa had tried to get an audience with him in the first place. Going above and beyond their initial deal, Jupiter then sent down a completely round shield to help keep the Roman people safe. Numa then had eleven copies of the shield made, all nearly identical but not quite. These twelve shields were referred to as the "ancilia" and became a sacred symbol to the city of Rome and its people.

Some scholars believe that this particular myth was meant both to teach the Roman people the traditional ways in which to worship Jupiter and to let them know that he would provide them with protection should they ask it of him.

The Origins of Rome

As mentioned in the previous chapter, the twin demigods, Romulus and Remus, were considered to be the founders of the city of Rome. The story goes that their maternal grandfather, King Numitor of Alba Longa, was overthrown by his brother, Amulius. Upon becoming king, Amulius exiled Numitor, killed his male heirs, and made his daughter, Rhea Silvia, a Vestal Virgin. As mentioned before, this meant she had to swear an oath of chastity, and to break it was punishable by death. At some point later, Mars came to Rhea Silvia (although some sources claim it may have been Hercules instead) and impregnated her. Upon the birth of the boys, King Amulius, too fearful of inciting the wrath of the boys' father, ordered their mother to be locked away and for the twins to be disposed of by a servant. What he ordered varied in different sources between being buried alive, thrown in the river Tiber, or left exposed to the elements. In all cases it was to be as a result of nature, not a man; and in every case the servant took pity on them and instead cast them down the river in a basket.

The river god Tibernus ensured the boys had a safe journey until they were caught on the roots or branches of a tree. It was said to be here that a she-wolf came across Romulus and Remus and decided to let them suckle on her for nourishment. Some claim that a woodpecker also provided them with food. After a short while more, the twins were then discovered by a shepherd who went on to raise the boys with his wife.

When Romulus and Remus had grown, they too worked as shepherds. When they came across some shepherds of King Amulius, a scuffle broke out and resulted in Remus being taken before the king. Romulus called upon his fellow local shepherds to help him save his brother. During the whole affair, King Amulius had no idea that these were the boys he had ordered to death, as he believed the deed had been done. In the ensuing events to save his brother, Romulus went on to defeat and kill King Amulius. The people were ecstatic and offered the two men the crown of Alba Longa. Instead they refused, reinstated their grandfather, and decided to go found their own city.

The downfall of the twin's relationship comes when they finally get close to choosing a location for their new city. Romulus wanted it on one hill, while Remus wanted it on another. They decide to let the birds decide, but even that method led to squabbling. In the end, Romulus started building in his preferred location. Remus continued to mock him for his choice, and most sources agree that it is Romulus who then kills him for it. Feeling remorseful, Romulus gives Remus the most honorific burial he can, and with that, Rome (Roma) is founded.

The Well-Remembered Stories of the Demigods

The well-renowned and strongest of the heroes of myth is none other than Hercules. In an unfortunate twist of fate, orchestrated by the jealous Juno, he killed his entire family, his wife and five children. Turning to the Oracle of Apollo, he was instructed to offer his services and strength to his cousin, the king of a nearby land. Juno played her hand once more, making sure that the tasks Hercules' cousin set for him were ones which everyone considered to be impossible to complete. Hercules went on to become known for the twelve labors he endured as a result. They involved the killing of: the Nemean lion, the Cretan bull, the Lernaean hydra, and the Stymphalian birds. There was also the capture of: the Erymanthian boar, the mares of Diomedes, the Keryenian hind, and the cattle of the Geryones. Other tasks included: stealing the girdle of Hippolyta, removing the apples of the Hesperides, and clearing out the Augean stables in a day. His final task was to capture the pet of Pluto and guardian of the underworld, Kerebos, a task deemed truly impossible but which he succeeds in, without the use of his strength. These were not the only deeds of Hercules, but they are his best known, and the ones that pushed him to the furthest reaches of his might as a hero.

Another well-remembered hero is Perseus. Again, like Hercules, he was—and still usually is—known for being a Greek hero. The Romans must have liked what they heard because, although there are less Roman texts about him, he still does seem to have been adopted into their mythology. The main myth surrounding him involves his successful slaying of the Gorgon Medusa, a supernatural woman, famous even in our culture today.

Next up, we have Castor and Pollux, who were the twin sons of Jupiter, via the mortal woman Leda. This also made them the half-brothers of Helen of Troy. They were also known as the Dioscuri, meaning "the youths of Zeus (Jupiter)." They had many temples dedicated in their honor. In some versions of the myth Castor was said to be mortal, while Pollux was immortal, as a result of Leda's husband, King Tyndareus, sleeping with her the same night Jupiter did. As the men grew they went on a variety of heroic adventures. The key one is the attempt to rescue their sister, Helen, after she is abducted by Theseus. In this myth, Castor and Pollux save their sister and then decide to kidnap Theseus' mother in return. In a later story, the twins take it upon themselves while out and about to abduct the daughters of Leucippus, Phoebe and Hilaeria. This results in a duel between Castor and Pollux, and the cousins of the girls, to whom they were already betrothed. In the end, Castor dies while Pollux survives. This is again where sources differ a little. Most seem to imply that Pollux shared his immortality with his brother, and as such was now tethered to the underworld. Other sources go on to say that Pollux was thus brought to be with the gods, and that the brothers alternate day by day as to who is in the underworld and who is in the immortal realm.

The Aeneid

Virgil's *Aeneid* is probably the most famous of the Roman myths. The story was written as twelve books, all in the form of a poem, and focuses around the life and deeds of the hero Aeneas. As mentioned previously, Aeneas was the son of Venus and was a survivor of the Trojan War. Virgil's story picks up at about the point where *The Iliad*, that famous Greek epic poem commonly attributed to Homer, leaves off. Aeneas fled for his life with other survivors as Troy burned, carrying his old and lame father Anchises on his back, with the hopes of settling a new home somewhere across the seas.

In the first six of the poetic books, we follow Aeneas as he spends time in Carthage, in the favor of Queen Dido, recounting the events of the Trojan War from the perspective of the Trojans. During his stay Dido falls in love with him, and he accepts her affections. This is, however, a ploy of Juno's, who wanted Troy to fall and does not want Rome to come into existence. Jupiter steps in when it seems that Aeneas will remain in Carthage for the remainder of his life, and reminds him of his mission to find the refugee Trojans their own, new home. Aeneas is renewed and once more sets sail. Dido is distraught and commits suicide. When Aeneas eventually sets foot on new soil, he is guided by a priestess of Apollo into the underworld. Here he learns from his deceased father that he has a great, fated task ahead of him and of Romulus and the wonder that Rome will become, provided he succeeds in his own time. He leaves the underworld with a more complete understanding of what he needs to achieve.

The second half of *The Aeneid* covers the settling of the Trojans and the resultant fighting from some neighboring kingdoms. Aeneas leads the Trojans to the region of Latium (where Alba Longa was also located—realistically, near modern day Naples) and settles there with the permission of the king of the area. Shortly, Aeneas begins courting the king's daughter, with the king's permission. Unfortunately, a nearby king, King Turnus, is also vying for the princess's hand and is supported in doing so by her mother. Eventually, it is Aeneas that marries the girl, but this pushes Turnus to arms. This is once more at the behest of Juno, who has chosen another way to try and prevent the formation of Rome. Outnumbered, Aeneas calls on fellow "Italians," the Tuscans and the Arcadians. Together they beat Turnus' forces back, but many lives are lost.

The mythological tale ends abruptly, with the final scenes depicting Aeneas killing Turnus in one-to-one combat. While this gives the story a dramatic end, it was likely not the intended ending. The issue is that Virgil died before he was able to finish the whole of the tale.

This myth played a large role in Roman culture for a vast majority of its existence and held a special power during the age of Augustus Caesar. It contributed to Augustus' own legacy as the modern-day Aeneas, the founder of a new Rome over 700 years after Romulus. It has been seen by many scholars as a way to get the Roman people to unlearn Greek habits. Not only that, but many Romans in positions of power would claim that their lineage came from Aeneas himself, in an attempt to convince the people that they were destined for higher office and a position of control over the masses.

The Passing On of Myths

Of course, there was a time when the myths of the Romans were not written down and were orally passed on. This is why elements vary from place to place and why what was considered to be *the* version could be altered slightly to fit the needs of the time and people. Even once many of the stories were put down on paper, it largely seems to have been by those that came in the latter part of the Roman period, basing a lot of their knowledge of the gods and how Romans would have acted upon their religion in the earlier days from hearsay and legends.

However, even the passing down of the mythological tales in these less reliable ways would have still meant a lot to the Romans of the time, as these stories held within them the essence of how the gods should be worshiped. This was of great importance to the Romans, who placed a high level of sanctity upon performing the rites of their religion in line with how their ancestors did.

The Importance of Telling Myths

The telling of mythological stories would have been important to the Romans on both a social and often political level. The point of the myths was to help people understand the natural events going on around them and how interdependent relationships work. Mythology is literally the root of each and every culture, and for the Romans it was no different. Mythology helps to create and maintain traditions. Through the retelling of myths, ancestors pass on information about the world and worship down through their descendants. It is no surprise therefore that mythology influenced everything from art and music, to the very language of a region itself. Not only that, but myths were a handy tool in keeping the peace both on large and small scales. Through giving the heroes attributes that help make someone a good or better person, people were more likely to strive to imitate that model within themselves. This would have helped keep communities together in every aspect, from not stealing from your neighbor, to going to war together to protect your collective livelihoods.

Chapter 4: The Influences of Greek Mythology on Roman Mythology

The commingling of these two major cultures and civilizations seemed to pick up its pace around 164 BC when the Romans invaded Greece a number of times. In all likelihood, there were already influences occurring long before this time, but this is the time period in which the evidence really starts to show. There are some scholars of ancient history who have claimed that the mixing of the Greek and Roman cultures, religion, and whatnot are a sign of the latter civilization being highly aware of their own cultural traits and therefore the benefits of others. There was also no hiding that the Greeks had a superior collection of literature to early Rome's, and a vast majority of that involved the tales of their gods. The result is that the Romans would have eagerly accepted the literature of the Greeks, to alter and adopt as their own.

The Romans were hardly the first to have done this, but they did nonetheless seem to be the most prolific in taking aspects from elsewhere, making all but a few alterations, and then claiming it as their own. The Romans truly were very proficient at this—taking more or less the whole stories and practices of the Greeks and then adding little elements that made them suddenly appear that these things had been Roman all along. Good examples of this are the tales of Aeneas and Hercules. Both of these demigods started out as Greek myths, but after the Romans saw how strong it would make them appear to imply that these heroes were of Roman origin instead, subtle but significant changes were quickly made. The main change that was easy to implement was to state that these demigods were of a more central Mediterranean background than the Greeks would have portrayed.

As mentioned above, the Romans were not the first to have stolen and adapted gods from another culture. In truth, numerous members of the Greek divine assembly were also based on gods and divine beings from other, even older cultures. The main difference between the way the Romans took on the gods as opposed to the Greeks is mostly in the details. Greeks had a way of making the gods "their own" in a way that the Romans didn't. This may have been because the two civilizations were already quite similar, leaving little they could actually make a change to aside from names.

The Similarities in Their Mythologies

Between the Romans and the Greeks, you hardly have to look closely in order to see just how similar their two mythologies are. In all honesty, the similarities between the two pop out at you the first moment you decide to take a look. That's a large part of the reason why so many of the similarities here are so vague or broad, while the differences are much more specific. For starters, Jupiter is basically the replica of the Greek King of the Gods, Zeus. The myth of his birth, who his siblings were, and whom he fathered are effectively identical, all apart from the names.

This was essentially the same for most of the gods, goddesses, and demigods. Regardless of whose story you choose to check out, you will always find that the main elements of their birth, including who their parents were and how they were conceived, all the way up to the deeds of their lives will be the same, with a few small of tweaks thrown in to help throw the lesser educated Roman off the scent. It probably didn't help matters that since the Romans took on so many Greek stories and didn't really have their own versions in place to begin with, they had little to go on except the Greek literature that was sitting tantalizingly before them, ready for the plucking.

A cultural similarity between the two mythologies comes from how the gods were worshiped in each. As will be mentioned in a moment, there were some differences here in terms of what they put more emphasis on, but the similarities are still plain to see. Both mythologies employed a variety of methods in which to worship their gods. In each culture there was the use of prayer, sacrifice, and annual festivals and games. It is probably due to the close links between the two cultures that the methods would have been so similar. Why change something if it works so well for others? Ultimately, the Greeks and Romans were human, and therefore routine, entertainment, and community would have been as crucial to their health and civility as it is to us today.

Another similarity between the two mythologies that doesn't seem to have changed even slightly is the names of the mortal mothers of the demigods. While in the case of heroes like Hercules the name of the hero may have been minorly altered, and in some other cases the place of birth replaced with something more Roman as opposed to significantly Greek, the names of the mothers of these heroic demigods seems to have gone largely unaltered. There are a few instances when the lineage of the mother is altered—perhaps she is suddenly no longer born of a Greek king, but a Roman hero—but in the majority of cases this is one step further than the Romans could be bothered to go in order to make a story their own. This is one of the main examples of how Greek mythology appears original, and the Roman version a copy. It lets the Roman front down, providing fairly definitive proof that the stories weren't theirs in the first place.

The Differences Between the Mythologies

While the similarities between the two mythologies tend to be quite broad and all-encompassing, the differences are, as a result, decidedly more focused and precise. One fairly noticeable difference between the two mythologies is the level of promiscuity and adultery enacted by the respective leading gods: Jupiter and Zeus. Where Zeus is said to have sired a vast range of gods, goddesses, and demigods, when you get down to crunching the numbers Jupiter just doesn't quite hold up. This does vary a little depending on the source, but for the most part Jupiter just didn't feel the need to be quite as sexually active as his Greek counterpart. There is no doubt that Jupiter still did plenty of sleeping around, but it does appear that a lot of the lovers and children that some scholars and sources try to attribute to him have little basis in ancient Roman artifacts. Often in these cases, the only suggestion that Jupiter could have done these things with these people is simply because it is recorded that Zeus did. It seems unconscionable to conflate the two mythologies beyond what the Romans did themselves. Therefore, without further Roman sources to prove that the many lovers of Zeus all copied over to become the lovers of Jupiter (the sort of evidence we do in fact have with so many other matters pertaining to mythological tales), we should assume that this was not necessarily the case.

Another of the main differences stems from before the two cultures would have had any significant mingling. This is the difference we mentioned before of the depiction of Neptune and Pluto as anything other than Jupiter's brothers. It appears that Neptune was the God of the Sea, or at least Freshwater, for the Romans even before any Greek influences arrived. The same goes for Pluto; he was most likely still considered the God of the Dead in early Roman religion. The significant change to becoming Jupiter's brothers would have only come once there was enough interactions between the Greeks and the Romans for the Romans to recognize the parallels between the divine counterparts. With the realization that in Greek culture Zeus, Poseidon (Neptune), and Hades (Pluto) together represented each key aspect of the world as a whole—the sky, the sea, and the underworld—it would have come quite naturally for the Romans to try and integrate this into their own myths since it implied their gods had more of a complete and unified control over the unimaginable power of the world itself.

One of the more minor differences between the two mythologies is visible when you take a look at the other supernatural beings present in the myths. While the Romans do still have some present, they seem to have taken the opportunity, where possible, to turn overly humanoid supernatural beings into simply minor gods or goddesses instead. The most noticeable example of this is the wife of Neptune. In Greek mythology, Poseidon's wife is a sea nymph, Amphitrite; in Roman mythology, however, she is Salacia, Goddess of Salt Water. In this case, since Amphitrite would have been eternally youthful and beautiful like a goddess, as a result of her being a nymph, it is not unreasonable to converge the two female supernatural types.

The other differences in the mythologies largely revolve around practices associated with the mythologies. Although the two cultures used primarily the same methods to worship their gods, the emphasis and importance of different methods did vary slightly. The Greeks seem to have slightly less need to perform private, home-based forms of worship. Instead they focused all their energy on making the public spectacles the most elaborate they could be. Additionally, they took the greatest pride in their annual games out of all their festivities. The Romans, on the other hand, focused a little more greatly on worshiping within the home in conjunction with their public honoring of the gods. One significant example pertains to the Roman household gods, the Lares, that were considered so important for pious Romans that Aeneas was depicted carrying their representative figurines out of destroyed Troy along with his father. And from the standpoint of public worship, the Romans treated nearly all their annual festivals with a balanced level of respect.

The fact that there are so few differences compared to similarities is hardly surprising, though. As stated before, the Romans had a good sense of culture and could appreciate when another culture's way of doing something was the superior option. This ability to adopt the actions of others as their own was likely key to their long-term success. On top of that, the Greeks and the Romans originated from very much the same area, particularly when compared on a global scale. Therefore, they would have encountered similar stimuli and had the same sort of interactions as each other, leading both cultures towards forming comparable societies and religions. The key reason it seems that the Romans would have taken a lot of their early religious cues from the Greek religion is simply because the Greek civilization was a tad older and therefore already a little more settled in their ways. And who could argue with the marvelous achievements of the Greek world?

So to recap, it isn't hard to notice that the mythology of Rome was largely based upon the mythology of Greece, or more specifically, that the majority of stories that the Romans chose to deem as the "official" tales of their Gods were never their tales in the first place.

Chapter 5: How the Gods Were Worshiped in Ancient Rome

What we call mythology, the Romans of the time would have recognized as their religion, just as the religions of today might one day die out and be deemed nonsensical. In fact, the Roman religion persisted for centuries and was only halted with the growth of Christianity in the Mediterranean. Even then it still managed to continue on in the privacy of many people's homes, found similar forms in paganism, and arguably saw elements co-opted by the Catholic Church. Without going any deeper, this is the obvious reason why the Romans would have worshiped their gods—because it was a religion and they did just as people all around the world do today. There has never really been a religion that did not have some form of worship at its core, so why would the Romans' be any different?

One grievance of Roman religion was that it was highly suspicious and manipulative in practice. Not only could it be used to manipulate the people, but those in power could alter the meaning of aspects of the religion itself in order to gain more favor among the Roman people and use it to gain advantages against their contemporaries and foes.

Not only did the Romans worship the Roman pantheon; they would also have a tendency to worship, or at least pray for, any mortals they knew who behaved in a manner befitting of a deity. This could have been people in positions of power but would have also included other, regular people, provided they expressed such qualities as kindness, morality, and honesty.

How the Gods Were Worshiped

There were multiple methods through which the Romans would show their veneration for their gods. The main ones were prayer, sacrifices, festivals, and other ritualistic activities. More often than not they would employ more than one method at a time. Another way they would have worshiped the gods was through the use of the Oracles. Oracles were consulted, most often by those in positions of power, to try and decipher what the gods deemed worthy of happening. More often than not, the prophecies which the oracles spewed would have been highly ambiguous so that in the end any outcome could be attributed to their words. However, it was still an important aspect of worship, as it showed fellow Romans that you wanted to get the gods' insight on your actions, and implied you held the greatest respect for their opinion. The practice of augury—a priest's inspection of a bird's entrails—satisfied a similar need in the lives of decision-makers, helping them discern whether a course of action was "auspicious" or "inauspicious."

Prayer, sacrifice, and rituals would have all followed particularly strict rules about how and when they were performed. In all cases, what was considered the correct way would have been passed down through the generations. This would have only added to the importance the Romans felt about performing these acts in the correct way. The Romans considered the respect of their ancestors as one of the most significant qualities to uphold within their society.

Religious festivities, on the other hand, had the opportunity to change as Rome itself did. Sometimes these alterations occurred in conjunction with the introduction of new gods or demigods from time to time. One example is the establishment of the Capitoline games, added to the annual festivities in honor of the significance that the Capitol and the Capitoline Triad (Jupiter, Juno, and Minerva) had for all Roman people. Generally speaking, though, it still would have taken a lot of persuasion and so-called divine evidence to prove that a change was acceptable and definitely approved of by the gods.

These events would require approval by the Senate or the Emperor, depending on which period of ancient Rome it happened within. This was because they were the only ones deemed to have the power to make such decisions, since it would have appeared that they were doing so on behalf of the gods.

Generally speaking, even these forms of worship would have been fairly fixed within the Roman culture; festivals and events were a major part of the Roman calendar and had fixed dates upon which they would fall. It was simply the case of when it was useful for the higher political offices to add or remove an element that they would find some major importance in order to permit themselves the change—while claiming it was all in line with the will of the gods.

Why Were They Worshiped?

The Romans worshiped their gods, goddesses, and demigods because they believed that through the worship of their deities they would receive all that they deserved. The ancient Roman religion was not all that different from any other religion in the sense that it revolved around there being mighty divine entities who could have an either negative or positive impact on your own life. It was considered natural then, much as it still is, to cling to the idea of a power greater than your own, in order to help the human mind make sense of things that it may otherwise struggle to make sense of. If you then believed that there were a whole assembly of beings with the ability to make your life either one of joy, or to destroy you at any time they pleased, would you not also want to pray to them often in order to win and maintain their favor?

Other reasons the Roman gods would have been worshiped included the pressures of political and powerful leaders throughout Roman society. These men would have made sure to put more emphasis on varying religious actions and activities, depending on what their own personal agenda was. Romans were naturally very superstitious due to their astute connections with their gods, and as such could rather easily be manipulated through that format. Therefore, it was common for people in power to leverage superstition and religious sincerity for their own ends. Some of those efforts brought benefits to the people as a whole; others primarily benefited the ones in power.

Remember how earlier in the book you were told to keep in mind how utterly entwined Roman religion was with all other aspects of Roman life? Well this is where it most significantly comes into play. Some historical figures were not so into all the religious goings on, and some even took down statues of some of the gods and goddesses, but these people were often either met with dissent and outrage from the masses or acted at odds to how they spoke on the matter. Cicero was one such example. Somewhat out-spoken about his dislike of highly religious activities, he was still one of the most influential when it came to enacting religious laws. In contrast, there was one particular emperor who took down a well-known statue of Juno within the city, and, to say the least, few people were unhappy to see him go when the time came. Fundamentally, if one wanted to stay in power, the best option usually involved the worship and public adoration of the gods.

Ultimately, the worship of the Roman gods was so integrated into what it meant to be a Roman that, coupled with the compelling admiration and generational respect the Romans had for their ancestors, it would have seemed like pure treason to deny their existence.

When Were They Worshiped?

Worshiping in Public

For the everyday people, worshiping in public would have been expected of them on sacred days. Outside of that, anyone could show public displays of worship as and when they pleased—perhaps at the birth of a first child, or to pray for good health for family members who were sick. It is of little surprise, given how eager Romans were to show off their displays of piety, that shrines and grottos were commonplace across Roman settlements. Not only that, but these locations would have allowed the people somewhere outside of their homes to easily display their offerings to the gods, in their eyes potentially increasing the likelihood of the gods taking notice.

For those in positions of power, worshiping in public and making it known that you were vying for the favor of a specific god or goddess would have been used to show where you stood on other matters—for example, how you were likely to act on major social concerns, or how likely you were to defend the lands against the city's foes. This would have helped to draw the attention and backing of specific groups, with which someone could gain a place in higher office. This was often reflected in the coinage of the era, with each new ruler giving homage to their chosen divine being, most likely as recognition for the god's or goddess's aid in securing their position.

Throughout the Roman period, but particularly under Cicero when he was the consul of the Roman Republic, religious activities and ceremonies were regarded at an elevated level compared to other social activities. Specific rites and ceremonies were to be performed on the correct dates and at the correct times, by all able people. If you were unsure of the ways to enact a particular rite or within a certain ceremony, then it was acceptable to ask an available priest for guidance on how to do so. This was in part acceptable due to the fact that Cicero bought in a law that would see anyone who failed to take part in the ceremonies punished and penalized for their inaction.

The necessity of publicly proving your worship was even clear in the architecture of the time. The most renowned structure in the entirety of Rome's lands was the Capitol, located at the heart of the city of Rome on the Capitoline Hill, right at the head of the

Roman Forum. This structure consisted of not only the political hub and seat of power for the nation, but also a selection of temples, including one each for Jupiter and Juno. On top of that, most, if not all, the buildings that made up the Capitol contained within their design, statues of numerous members of the Roman pantheon. With such an impressive and influential structure being home simultaneously to such high-profile religious elements, we can see the innate necessity of the Romans to always be worshiping their gods and can more easily understand how this would have so readily trickled down into every aspect of ancient Roman life.

And today, visitors to Rome can still walk inside the breathtaking domed structure known as the Pantheon, a temple erected in honor of all the gods by Agrippa, the highly respected lieutenant of Augustus, as part of the renewal program instituted by the pious emperor.

Worshiping in Private

Private worship, though not directly supported by the government and the Roman priesthood, played a vital role as the foundation of public worship. Had there not been traditions and rites evolving within the home, there never would have been the public option to display them. In private, the Roman people were expected to enact the correct rites and ceremonies on the correct days. As with public ceremonies, if someone was unsure of the proper way to follow through with a particular rite or ceremony you were permitted to check with a priest from a relevant cult. However, in most cases, rites performed in private would have been based on the way it was performed by their ancestors and as such, one would know how to perform them from it being passed down to them throughout their youth.

Worshiping in private was of great importance to the Romans for two main reasons. First, worshiping in the home centered the whole experience around prayer with, and for, your family. Since family was a core aspect of the Roman culture and lifestyle, common people would have incorporated the two aspects, using the time for private prayer to ensure that some family time was had. The other important part of worshiping in private is that it was an opportunity to invite gods and goddesses in and ask them to bless the house, the family within it, and their wider relatives by proxy.

It is unlikely that when it came to worshiping in private there would have been many sacrifices performed. This does not mean that they didn't happen, but it would have been easier to save the more hardcore method of worship for major events when there would have been more hands available for both the act and the clean-up. In the privacy of one's own home, all Romans would have tended to focus on prayer in order to express to their gods their concerns, thanks, and favor. Burning of incense or other modest types of offerings would regularly accompany these petitions.

Each household was equipped with their own altar. It was called the "lararium" and would be worshiped at by those living in the house twice every day. One prayer would be said in the morning, the other in the evening. This form of worship would be practiced by all those residing in the home. Outside of these two daily occasions, any member could use the altar to pray independently and perhaps provide small offerings for specific situations. The deities that would have been focused on during private prayer were the gods of the house (physical structure) and the patron god or goddess of the family.

The worship of the Roman pantheon was such a core part of so many Romans' historical and social identity that for years beyond the ban of public displays of worship to these gods—replaced with the rites and expectations of Christianity in the region—many still took the time out every day to pray to their patron Roman deities.

Why and When Would a Specific God Be Worshiped?

The Romans had a god or goddess for nearly everything, and each of those would tend to have a very specific function over which they would preside. The Romans often went to the extreme in this sense; a good example of just how particular the Romans could be is through the example of how they would worship the gods of their homes. They had a god for guarding the door to their home, but not only that. There were also separate gods for the threshold, hinges, and other distinctly named parts of the door as a whole. When worshiping, the Romans would have tended to pray to Forculus (God of Doors), or Cardea (Goddess of Hinges), since these were deemed to be the most useful parts of the doorway. However, given the Romans' naturally superstitious tendencies, they were unlikely to have ignored the other gods completely.

On a larger scale, gods and goddesses would have been worshiped based on whether they suited the needs of the worshiper. Such situations may have been worshiping Neptune at times when one was about to go fishing or before setting out on long, sea voyages. Other times worship would have occurred while performing with phallic objects of Mutunus Tutunus during marriage rites or praying to Mars and Victoria specifically on the eve of war, and at the time of success, respectively.

A vast majority of Roman religious festivals would have been dedicated to a specific god or goddess. One of the examples of this that has already been mentioned are the festivals of Ceres. Neptune also had a festival dedicated to him, Neptunalia. This took place in late July—just in time for when the risk of drought would reach its peak. Often, with these festivals, the intention was to draw the god's attention to the matter happening in the mortal realm, in the hope of some assistance in the (usually seasonal) circumstances that were to come.

Chapter 6: Where You Can Still See Roman Mythology's Influence Today

Spotting Roman Mythology in Modern Western Society

When you start to look for the mention of Roman gods and goddesses in modern society and culture you will be surprised by just how many references you will ultimately find. For starters, there are the more obvious examples, namely the planets of our solar system (although admittedly most were not named in "modern" times) and the subsequent naming of many of NASA's explorations into space—the Apollo missions being the most famous. In fact not only are all the planets (except Earth) of the solar system named after the Roman gods, but a vast number of those planets' moons are too. When we look among the satellites of our neighboring space, we have given them names including the likes of Metis, Titan, Rhea, and Dione. Many of the other moons have received names from Greek mythology, but for the most part it is a varied mix of the two, regardless of the planet they are orbiting. In more recent years, with Pluto being demoted to a dwarf planet, we have actually gained some others as dwarf planets too. A major one of these was already called Ceres, residing within the asteroid belt between Mars and Jupiter, and at least now the god and goddess are deemed on par with each other!

The other presence of Roman mythology in modern society is the obvious one—the depiction of the myths and culture in our media. From the many varying adaptations of *Hercules* to the film *Troy*, it is clear that people today still have a hankering for hearing these stories of heroes and gods and the fantastical lives they lived. Our fascination in this, and other, historical religions stems from the very essence of our humanity. Humans are naturally both curious and sentimental beings. As a result, we like to look back at our ancestors and delve into the ways in which we are still the same, as well as the ways that have drastically changed.

In Modern Language

In a likewise manner, more than a few of our words and names have stemmed from Roman mythological influences. Words as simple as "cereal" and "atlas" have direct connections with the Roman gods and goddesses. "Cereal" dates back to a meaning "of Ceres," who you will remember as the goddess of agriculture and grain. And the name Ceres itself is based on the latin root that means "to feed." A more direct example comes in the form of "atlas." Atlas was the Titan who, after fighting with the other Titans against the gods, was punished with the task of bearing the heavens and the earth upon his shoulders. That image seemed a fitting cover for printed collections of maps during the Renaissance, and thus "the Atlas" came to signify the book of maps that had his image on its cover.

Finally, names. It will be of little surprise to learn that many names we hear all the time even now stem back to ancient civilizations; it's a natural progression based on the origins of our very language! Regardless of that, though, what may in fact surprise you are some of the names that have their origins in ancient Roman times. Names including "Felix" and "Camilla" first appear in the Roman period, despite having (considered by some) a very "modern" sound to them.

In addition to those, we also see outright, historically Roman words and names dotted throughout our culture. "Pluto" is the name used for a dog by Disney, and there are also examples in the names of foods, such as *caesar* salad. Interestingly enough, it is believed in more recent times that "caesar" (which, to clarify, was a title, not a name) was perhaps pronounced more along the lines of the German word "kaiser" and the Russian word "tsar" and was in fact the precursor for these titles, even though they are not heavily Latin-rooted languages. And so, we can see that such ancient influences directly feed into our common tongue even today.

Everyday Examples

However, the moment you turn your eyes towards looking for more examples, they easily start to pop out. One fairly major example is from the goddess Venus. As mentioned previously, Venus is the goddess of love and is also treated as being synonymous with beauty. As a result we tend to see the word "venus" or the depiction of a beautiful lady referred to as Venus in multiple different cultural forms, from art to music. Not only that, but the name Venus has also been used by companies to invoke in the masses the idea of particular beauty standards, connecting for example the name with the likes of female safety razors in order to imply to women that this is a product that would aid them in increasing their own individual beauty.

Another ordinary example can be found in the world of chocolate bars. The Mars Bar. Not always in circulation in the USA, this chocolate bar is sold globally and is clearly a moniker of the ancient Roman god of war. In this case there seems to be less of a connection to what the god represented, but who knows, maybe the original creator wanted to "go to war" with other chocolate bar providers for the recognition as the best chocolate bar on the market.

In some instances, Roman gods and goddesses are still being used by modern cultures to indicate their successes and aspirations. One such example of this is the statue of Victoria (the Roman goddess of victory), atop the Berlin Victory Column. In this instance the presence of this goddess is for the same reason that the Romans would have erected statues and temples in her honor—to commemorate a successful war. What's more, since these names and depictions tend to be chosen due to the connotations of the one being portrayed, the fact that we then as a society are able to immediately react and understand the intentions of the song, artwork, or company, shows that the presence of these Roman mythological figures are that ingrained in our modern society that we barely blink an eye.

Conclusion

So to conclude: based on all you have read here, it should now be clear why the mythology of Ancient Rome is such a highly interesting topic to so many people even these two centuries, and more, later. Hopefully your understanding of mythology and the Romans has grown and you now have a solid basis of information safely tucked away to draw or expand upon in the future.

By now you should have a solid understanding of who the gods of the Roman pantheon were. As stated at the beginning, the name Jupiter alone has come up on more occasions than it is worth counting. Jupiter could never be forgotten in the context of Rome, as the two of them essentially exist because of each other, and—unlike the Greeks who did not choose the power of the King of the Gods for their capital—Jupiter was the patron god of the whole city, and eventually the Empire. Similarly, those with the names of our planets and additional representations in modern media (Neptune, Pluto, Venus being the key ones) will not be forgotten any time soon. Ideally, with the knowledge you have now read, you'll remember them even more assuredly. The best outcome of this book would certainly be that you finish it with the names of new gods swirling around your head and an eagerness to read up on them more just raring to go.

If, as time passes after you have finished reading, you struggle to recall the reasons for why the demigods existed, simply remember that they were generally considered the epitome of man, with a few flaws thrown in to keep them seeming human. The point of the myths surrounding heroes like Aeneas, Hercules, and Romulus and Remus was not only to give some backstory and originality to the culture, but also to remind the citizens what it means to be good people. More than the gods ever could be, demigods were supposed to be the image of a perfect citizen, what would come to mind when Romans thought of what they aspired to be like.

If this book has managed to succeed in what it set out to do, you will now have a significant understanding of how the Romans worshiped, the differences between the ways they worshiped in public and the ways they worshiped in private, and—most importantly—why it is that they worshiped these divine beings. It is a marvel to think that so many cultures, all the way up to modern times, put so much faith and effort into creating a connection with beings that, if they ever have existed, will unlikely be seen by a regular person in their lifetime. The main thing to remember is that the culture that the Romans experienced was very different from our own and therefore many of the ways they expressed their honor and worship to their gods was nothing like what we see most places today. However, for the time and place, the Romans were pretty standard in their practices compared to their contemporaries around the globe.

By now you should have come across at least one mythological tale that really took your fancy. Perhaps you were won over by the defeat of the Titans by Jupiter and his siblings and now you want to learn more about what the world of the Titans was like. Otherwise maybe the mention of the labors of Hercules has meant that you are now planning on reading the stories detailing the deeds themselves. What's even better is there is a whole world of Roman myths out there that haven't even been mentioned here. And once you're done with those you can move on to the Greeks or the Egyptians or so many others! Just remember, from time to time you'll suddenly realize you've read this story somewhere else before, as it is almost impossible to be original when you're all talking about more or less the same gods.

Had you realized how heavily the Romans were influenced by the Greeks? Were any of the similarities, or maybe one or two of the differences, not something you expected? That is part of what makes mythology such a wonderful aspect of history to cover. It allows you to see what the culture of a whole time period may have been like just through letting you make these connections between different groups at the time.

Hopefully you will not only have learned many new things, but some of the things you knew before will have been further expanded on. Plus, maybe you are now much more aware of the presence of Roman mythology in our day-to-day life. You may even find that these things will continue to stand out to you in the world around you, long after you have finished reading this book.

Roman mythology is something that should absolutely be dived right in to and enjoyed. Thank you for taking the time to read this book. I hope you have enjoyed it!

References

Anderson, W.S. (n.d.). *Aeneas*. Britannica. www.britannica.com/topic/Aeneas

Apel, T. (n.d.). *Jupiter*. Mythopedia. mythopedia.com/roman-mythology/gods/jupiter/

Apel, T. (n.d.). *Neptune*. Mythopedia. mythopedia.com/roman-mythology/gods/neptune/

Apel, T. (n.d.). *Pluto*. Mythopedia. mythopedia.com/roman-mythology/gods/pluto/

Braun, E. (2019). *Roman myths*. Raintree.

Cartwright, M. (2016, June 10). *Castor and Pollux*. Ancient History Encyclopedia. www.ancient.eu/Castor_and_Pollux/

Cartwright, M. (2012, July 9). *Hercules*. Ancient History Encyclopedia. www.ancient.eu/hercules/

Cassius, D., & Scott-Kilvert, I. (1987). *The Roman history : the reign of Augustus*. Penguin Books.

Chisholm, K., & Ferguson, J. (1981). *Rome : the Augustan Age*. Oxford University Press, In Association With The Open University Press.

Clayton, E. (n.d.). *Cicero (106-43 B.C.E)*. Internet Encyclopedia of Philosophy. iep.utm.edu/cicero/

Cole, W.F. (2014, August 17). *The Aeneid.* Ancient History Encyclopedia. www.ancient.eu/The_Aeneid/

Crawford, M. (1992). *The Roman republic.* Fontana.

Garcia, B. (2018, April 18). *Romulus and Remus.* Ancient History Encyclopedia. www.ancient.eu/Romulus_and_Remus/

Gill, N.S. (2017, June 19). *You already know Greek myths.* ThoughtCo. www.thoughtco.com/you-already-know-greek-myths-111773

Grant, M. (n.d.). *Roman religion.* Britannica. www.britannica.com/topic/Roman-religion

Graves, R. (1992). *The Greek myths.* Penguin Books.

Greek Gods and Goddesses. (2017, February 22). *Jupiter.* greekgodsandgoddesses.net/gods/jupiter/

Kelly, L. (2019, July 2). *Why Greek and Roman gods are so similar.* History 101. www.history101.com/similarities-roman-greek-gods/

Mark, J.J. (2018, October 31). *Mythology.* Ancient History Encyclopedia. www.ancient.eu/mythology/

NovaRoma. (2012, November 26). *Household worship.* www.novaroma.org/nr/Household_Worship

Roman Worship. (n.d.). *Worship of significant gods.* romanworship.weebly.com/worship-of-significant-gods.html

Speicher, C. (n.d.). *The importance of mythology.* The Odyssey Online. www.theodysseyonline.com/the-importance-of-mythology

Tales Beyond Belief. (2017). *Jupiter.* www.talesbeyondbelief.com/roman-gods/jupiter.htm

Tales Beyond Belief. (2017). *Roman Gods.* www.talesbeyondbelief.com/roman-gods/roman-gods-index.htm

Wasson, D.L. (2014, May 6). *Jupiter.* Ancient History Encyclopedia. www.ancient.eu/jupiter/

Willis, K. (2020, December 23). *Who were the Romans?* WiseGeek. www.wisegeek.com/who-were-the-romans.htm

www.ingramcontent.com/pod-product-compliance
Lightning Source LLC
LaVergne TN
LVHW011740060526
838200LV00051B/3266